Principles of Christian Morality

HEINZ SCHÜRMANN
JOSEPH CARDINAL RATZINGER
HANS URS VON BALTHASAR

Principles of Christian Morality

Translated by Graham Harrison

IGNATIUS PRESS   SAN FRANCISCO

Title of the German original:
Prinzipien Christlicher Moral
© 1975 Johannes Verlag
Einsiedeln, Switzerland

Cover by Victoria Hoke Lane

With ecclesiastical approval
© 1986 Ignatius Press, San Francisco
All rights reserved
ISBN 0–89870–086–8
Library of Congress catalogue number 85–82176
Printed in the United States of America

Contents

Preface

Nowadays the question of the content and basis of the Christian ethos is becoming more and more prominent in theology; more than other problems, it touches the very nerve of the Christian life. It was this situation that caused the International Theological Commission, after years of preparatory work, to grapple with the issue in its December 1974 session. Many pieces of mosaic, as it were, were collected on that occasion, but they could not be assembled into a whole; here, two of those pieces are presented to the public.

For years, in his capacity as a member of the subcommittee responsible for moral questions, Heinz Schürmann has worked on the issue of the New Testament's contribution on ethical matters. After exhaustive discussion, the Commission adopted in general terms the results of his research on the question of the normative nature of New Testament values and precepts. Hans Urs von Balthasar presents nine theses outlining the fundamental data of Christian morality and shows its inner logic within the broad context of anthropology and the history of the basic forms of ethics. Balthasar's framework was accepted by the Commission. Joseph Ratzinger's contribution appeared originally as a series of articles in *L'Osservatore*

Romano, and it is not directly connected with the work of the Commission. However, since it takes up some of the same lines as the works of the other two writers, it seemed worthwhile to include it here. It was necessary to keep the compass of the book within strict limits, and thus it proved impossible to include other studies undertaken by the subcommittee, so ably led by Monsignor Philippe Delhaye.

We, the joint authors—none of whom is a specialist in moral theology—are well aware of the fragmentary nature of what we have written, which is by no means intended to detract from the detailed work of the specialists, let alone render it superfluous. Yet it must be said that the great fundamental questions of theology never fit neatly into the specialists' categories; they always need to be discussed in open forum. What would become of dogmatics without the interventions and observations of scriptural exegetes? And how could exegesis pursue its path without philosophical and theological reflection on its governing principles? So we hope that, precisely because we come to the fundamental issues of moral theology from other disciplines, we may have a contribution to make to a question which, after all, affects the whole of both theology and faith.

The Authors
Easter 1975

HEINZ SCHÜRMANN

How Normative Are the Values and Precepts of the New Testament?
A Sketch[1]

[1] These theses were laid before the Plenary Session of the International Theological Commission in December 1974 and were approved by it *"in forma generica ut textus CTI"*. I am grateful for what I have learned from some of the contributions to the discussion and some of the solutions proposed. Otherwise, the theses have only been slightly improved stylistically.

The issue

The Second Vatican Council has "opened the treasures of the Bible more lavishly so that a richer fare may be provided for the faithful at the table of God's word";[2] the Holy Scriptures become the "word of life" (*viva vox*) when "by means of the homily the mysteries of the faith and the guiding principles of the Christian life are expounded. . . ."[3] For "the divinely revealed realities, which are contained and presented in the text of sacred Scripture, have been written down under the inspiration of the Holy Spirit . . . they have God as their author. . . ." Therefore "the ministry of the Word . . . is healthily nourished and thrives in holiness through the Word of Scripture."[4] "And such is the force and power of the Word of God that it can serve the Church as her support and vigor, and the children of the Church as strength for their faith, food for the soul, and a pure and lasting fount of spiritual life."[5] "What was handed on by the apostles comprises everything that serves to make the People of God live their lives in holiness and increase their faith."[6] This view of Holy Scripture,

[2] *Sacrosanctum Concilium* 51; cf. *Dei Verbum* 22.
[3] Ibid. 52; cf. *Dei Verbum* 24.
[4] *Dei Verbum* 24.
[5] Ibid., 21.
[6] Ibid., 8.

which sees it as "the soul, as it were, of all theology",[7] explains why, in giving "special care" to "the perfecting of moral theology", the Church desires that the latter's "scientific presentation should draw more fully on the teaching of Holy Scripture."[8]

Postconciliar moral theology, however, seems to be concerned less with ecclesiological issues than with tasks in the world, less with "throwing light upon the exalted vocation of the faithful in Christ" than with "their obligation to bring forth fruit in charity for the life of the world".[9] Thus, instead of building up a "community ethos", moral theology is now seeking to solve world problems; consequently, it devotes itself to a rational exposition of the norms of practical action rather than to the spiritual elucidation of Scripture. All the same, the two are not opposed; moral theology can rightly claim the support of Vatican II as it pursues these programs in the world, for the Council affirms that moral theology has a "missionary aspect",[10] and that the forms of the apostolate should take into account "the human conditions, not merely spiritual and moral but also social, demographic and economic".[11] The "Pastoral Constitution on

[7] *Optatam totius* 16; cf. *Dei Verbum* 24.
[8] *Optatam totius* 16.
[9] Ibid.
[10] *Ad gentes* 39.
[11] *Christus Dominus* 17.

the Church in the Modern World" urges us[12] to show solidarity with mankind today in its searchings and to endeavor to provide encouragement in terms of values and pointers in the various spheres of life. This must not be done merely in a general way: we must cooperate in finding just, applicable and detailed norms of practical action. Such a ministry on the part of moral theology is definitely a genuine work of the apostolate and of charity. Yet it cannot draw more than heretofore on the ethical statements of Holy Scripture, for they simply do not envisage many of the concrete questions concerning mankind today. If we realize that not only the books of the Old Testament "contain matters imperfect and provisional",[13] but also those of the New (see the following discussion), we must face the question of how far Holy Scripture and how far experience—that is, ethical reason—are competent to discover what is right action, in terms both of principles and of detailed applications.

Do not the imperfect and provisional ethical pronouncements that are met with in Holy Scripture lend weight to the view that, so far as their claim to binding validity is concerned, they are dependent upon extrinsic rational substantiation? This is

[12] *Gaudium et spes* (passim).
[13] *Dei Verbum* 15.

surely the case with the values and precepts of Scripture in matters peculiar to Israel's life. Must we not be very much aware, when dealing with the biblical writers, of a historically determined obfuscation of the ethical consciousness on the one hand, and of a constantly changing historical situation on the other, with the result that neither general ethical values nor concrete precepts and instructions can claim abiding validity, let alone absolute validity? If we do hold on to this absolute validity, are we not obliged to say that the biblical precepts, instructions and exhortations are only valid beyond their time as "paradigms" or as "models" of behavior— which would mean that, ultimately, ethical evaluation lies with human experience and ethical reason, not with the utterances of Holy Scripture? We must take questions such as these seriously. (Here, of course, we cannot provide solutions, but, at most, shed light on certain relevant aspects.[14])

---

[14] Here we can only indicate the New Testament basis; for more detail cf. the following: (1) H. Schürmann, "Die Gemeinde des Neuen Bundes als der Quellort des sittlichen Erkennens nach Paulus", in *Catholica* 26 (1972): 15–37. (2) H. Schürmann, " 'Das Gesetz des Christus' (Gal 6:2). Jesu Verhalten und Wort als letztgültige sittliche Norm nach Paulus", in *Neues Testament und Kirche* (*Festschrift für R. Schnackenburg*) (Freiburg-Basle-Vienna, 1974) (also available in a slightly fuller form in H. Schürmann, *Jesu ureigener Tod.*

The question of the binding nature of biblical values and precepts is ultimately a question of the application of *hermeneutics* in moral theology. This also involves the question of *exegesis*; that is, what kind of binding quality the biblical writings claim or evince.

"The books of the Old Testament . . . divinely inspired, preserve a lasting value . . ." (Rom 15:4).[15] "God . . . in his wisdom has so brought it about that the New should be hidden in the Old and that the Old should be made manifest in the New" (Augustine, *Quaest.*, in *Hept.* 2, 73: PL 34, 623).[16] Consequently, in what follows we shall limit ourselves to the writings of the New Covenant, since "the books of the Old Testament, all of them caught up into the gospel message, attain and show forth their full meaning in the New Testament",[17] and since the question of the binding validity of the biblical values and precepts stands

---

Exegetische Besinnungen und Ausblicke [Freiburg, 1974], 97–120). (3) H. Schürmann, "Haben die paulinischen Wertungen und Weisungen Modellcharakter? Beobachtungen und Anmerkungen zur Frage nach ihrer formalen Eigenart und inhaltlichen Verbindlichkeit", in *Gregorianum* 56 (1975): 237–271.

[15] *Dei Verbum* 14.
[16] Ibid., 16.
[17] Ibid., 16.

or falls by the New Testament writings. We must bear in mind, of course, that the New Testament writings—in spite of their astonishing diversity of ethical conceptions (e.g., those of Paul, John, Matthew, James and so forth)—have much in common so far as our question is concerned; they are all rooted in the extensive tradition of the primitive Church. It is universally recognized that the constellation of ethical problems is subjected to very special reflection in Paul's thought; therefore, in what follows, the question at issue is illustrated by reference to the Pauline values and precepts.

The New Testament writings can claim their values and precepts to be specially normative because they document the ethical stance of the "original" Church, which, since she was in the process of becoming, was still receiving revelation (cf. Eph 2:20 and 3:5) and was being molded in an exceptional way by the Spirit of the risen Lord (cf. Acts 11:15). "The apostolic preaching . . . is expressed in a special way in the inspired books";[18] the apostles handed on "what they themselves had received" (cf. Heb 2:3)—from the tradition of the primitive Christian communities and ultimately from the Lord himself.

[18] Ibid., 8.

So far as Paul's values and precepts are concerned (cf. 1 Cor 7:10, 25 and 7:12, 40), we can distinguish two groups: (1) The words and deeds of Jesus yielded ultimately binding precepts—which were perceived, in the post-Easter experience, as coming from the risen Lord; and (2) the values and precepts (stamped by the words and deeds of Jesus) of the apostles, of other primitive Christian pneumatics and of the various traditions handed down in the primitive Christian communities. This Pauline distinction provides us with a framework for the observations that follow.

I

Jesus' Deeds and Words as the Ultimate Ethical Norm

For the New Testament writers, Jesus' deeds and words provide a standard of values, an ultimate ethical norm. They are the "law of Christ" (Gal 6:2) that has been accepted as the norm in the hearts of believers (cf. 1 Cor 9:21). The New Testament writers definitely see the pre-Easter instructions of Jesus in the context of a binding teaching—and of a binding demand for discipleship—which arises from the conduct of the earthly Jesus—and even more from that of the pre-existent Son of God.

The whole behavior of Jesus, interpreted in the light of his words, is the "law of Christ" (Gal 6:2); it has the character of ultimate precept and yields an "accord with Christ Jesus" (Rom 15:5), the "mind of Christ Jesus" (Phil 2:5). "In Christ Jesus", however, the heteronomous "law" becomes an autonomous norm: the believer is a person in whom the law of Christ has been implanted as a normative principle (cf. 1 Cor 9:21), who has "the mind of Christ" (1 Cor 2:16) because "the truth of Christ" is in him (2 Cor 11:10). At the same time the various New Testament writings give quite different emphases to kerygma and precept, indicative and imperative pronouncements.

Somehow or other, New Testament exhortation is always to be found in the framework—or rather at the focus—of christological formulas of faith (cf., e.g., Phil 2:6–11, 1–5). Ultimately, even Jesus' pre-Easter actions can only be understood on the basis of his word—just as, conversely, his pre-Easter teaching has to be understood in the light of his pre-Easter conduct and attitude. It is Jesus' consciousness of being the "one who has come", the "Son"—an awareness that informs his actions and his whole attitude—that illuminates his announcement of the "nearness" of the Kingdom of God, as well as what he says of the "Father's" love, which seeks out sinners. Even when the post-Easter writings place more emphasis on the challenging words of Jesus (thus the Synoptic Gospels and sources) or on apostolic exhortation (e.g., the Letter of James, the Pastoral Epistles), they place them in the context of the summons to discipleship and imitation issued by the "one who has come", the "Son"; that is, the crucified and risen "Christos". Paul, the First Letter of Peter and (in a different way) John stress the exemplary conduct of Jesus so strongly that, by contrast, they give scant attention, or at least little space, to his ethical teaching. Let us then consider (1) Jesus' conduct and (2) Jesus' words separately.

1. The Conduct of Jesus
as an example and standard of a ministering and self-surrendering love

In the New Testament writings, Jesus' conduct is ultimately shown as a ministering and self-surrendering love "for us", as a "pro-existent" love which gets involved, making God's "pro-existence" ("for us") visible in an eschatological manner (e.g., Rom 5:8; 8:31ff. and Jn 3:16; 1 Jn 4:9). By receiving and accepting this eschatological love of God, which allows itself to be communicated, and by imitating it and handing it on in a life which is with Christ and in Christ, that the moral lives of believers are fundamentally shaped.

As early as the synoptic account, the coming of Jesus, his life and his activity, is understood as service (Lk 22:27f.), coming to a climax in the surrender of death (Mk 10:45). In the pre-Pauline and Pauline writings this love is interpreted kenotically as a love that is fulfilled in the "Son's" Incarnation and death on the Cross (cf. Phil 2:6ff.; 2 Cor 8:9), and in Johannine terms as a love that reaches its "accomplishment" (Jn 19:28, 30) in the "descent" of the "Son of Man" in Incarnation and death (Jn 6:41f., 48–51 passim), in the purifying death service (Jn 13:1–11)—as the completion of Jesus' "work" (Jn 17:4; cf. 4:34).[19]

a. In the New Testament writings—particularly in Paul and John—the commandment of love (over and above its eschatological thrust) acquires its motivation, and hence its distinctiveness, its self-transcending radicality and even perhaps a specific content from the self-emptying (Paul) or self-abasing (John) attitude of the Son (the Son of Man), especially as this love that enters into human existence and death represents and illustrates the love of God.

While it is certainly true that the New Testament commandment of love draws its distinctiveness and radicality from eschatology, which provides a future-oriented motivation for the Christian life (particularly in the pre-Easter preaching of Jesus), ultimately this distinctiveness and radicality come from the fact that the eschaton has already broken through into our world with the coming of Jesus— and definitively with Jesus' death and resurrection. Thus, the loving assimilation of Jesus' life and death of service on the part of his disciples must also be seen as the breakthrough of the eschaton.

The love of God that manifests itself in the Incarnation and death of Jesus is portrayed—

---

[19] Cf. the article mentioned in note 14 (2).

particularly by Paul and John—as being qualitatively different; it cannot be understood in terms of human self-renunciation or "humility". Consequently, the challenge to imitate this love,[20] to join the company of the Crucified and to become like him,[21] must be a distinctive element of New Testament ethics. It will be neither intelligible nor feasible from the point of view of secular ethics, and hardly more so from the perspective of a transcendental/religious ethics external to Christian faith.

b. Discipleship and imitation of the incarnate and crucified Jesus, being a member of his "company", and the life of the baptized in Christ impart a characteristic quality to the human/ethical behavior *of believers in the world, over and above the commandment of love.*

This distinctive christological element shapes the whole ethical behavior of believers ever more widely. It explains the summons to a self-renunciation that goes to the extreme of martyrdom (Mk 8:35 passim), the command to love one's enemies (cf. Mt 5:43–47), to renounce one's rights (cf., e.g., 1 Cor 6:1–8), not to countenance divorce

[20] Cf. Phil 1:3ff.; 2 Cor 8:9; Rom 15:2f., 7; Col 3:13; Eph 5:1f.; Heb 12:1f.; 13:11f.; 1 Jn 3:16.

[21] Cf., e.g., Mk 8:34ff.; 9:33–37; Phil 3:10; Gal 6:14; 2 Cor 12:10; 1 Pet 2:22–25.

(Mk 10:2–12; 1 Cor 7:10f.). It also facilitates and colors the characteristic Christian relationship to the world, which is both distanced and involved (cf. 1 Cor 7:29ff.) and calls for voluntary self-denial and poverty (cf. 2 Cor 6:4–10), separation from family (Lk 14:26), and celibacy (cf. Mt 19:12; 1 Cor 7). Ultimately, the whole approach of believers is governed and radically shaped by this central core.

2. The Words of Jesus
as the ultimate ethical norm

The Lord's words interpret the loving actions of Jesus, the One who has come, the Crucified. Without them, Jesus' actions would not be intelligible. But it is equally true that the Lord's words must be understood by reference to the pre-Easter conduct of Jesus, and ultimately from the mystery of the Incarnation and the Paschal mystery (see the previous discussion). In the light of this twofold mystery, "called to mind" in the Spirit (cf. Jn 14:26), they are the final norm of ethical behavior for believers, as Paul says explicitly in 1 Corinthians 7:10f., 25. But this had also been emphasized by the presynoptic tradition and the Gospels, which presented the communities and believers with a rule of life, a

*community rule, in the form of "the sayings of Jesus"—
the Jesus who had "come" and "been delivered up"—
and thus enjoined upon them a binding code of conduct.*

Even prior to Easter, the words of Jesus are illuminated by his actions, just as, conversely, what
he does must be understood by what he says, as
we have made clear. Since, however, the actions
of Jesus only reached their fulfillment in his return
to the Father, in his death and resurrection (exalta-
tion), the Lord's words can only be understood
fully after Easter (cf. Jn 3:11f.). Thus they are
established as normative in the form in which the
Church of the apostolic age handed them on, that
is, in the New Testament writings, where we can
often see how they have been fitted into the new
context. Furthermore, it is the Spirit of the risen
Lord which "transforms" these words in that new
situation (cf. Jn 14:25f.; 16:13ff.).

*a. The words of Jesus may be held to be the ultimate
ethical norm; yet we must attend to their literary character.
Most of the words of Jesus, as their literary character
reveals, are not intended to be understood as "laws".
Many of them are clearly* models of conduct, *that is,
they are intended as paradigms.*

We can see this paradigmatic character of Jesus'
words from time to time in his metaphorical pro-

nouncements (cf. Lk 6:41f.), his casuistic examples (cf. Lk 6:29f.) or in the apparent paradoxes in which he puts commandments in an extreme form (cf. Mt 5:21f., 27f., 33–34a, 37). A great number of the Lord's words are intended to convince and motivate the hearer in the sense of religious/ethical wisdom.

b. We must go on to ask whether any of the Lord's words are intended to have a "legal" validity, in a rabbinic sense. At any rate Paul, the rabbinic scholar, does not understand them in this way, no doubt because, fundamentally, he interprets them within the perspective of Jesus' loving "self-emptying" and "humiliation" (see the previous discussion). In the two instances in which he expressly reproduces commands on the part of Jesus (cf. Lk 10:7b parr and Mk 10:11f. parr), he urges his addressees to follow the commands of Jesus—in their changed and thus more difficult situation—not in a late Jewish, legalistic way, but by endeavoring to embrace the intention behind them (cf. 1 Cor 9:14 on the one hand and 7:12–16 on the other).[22]

Paul does not understand Luke 10:7b as a command to be carried out, but—in the changed circumstances—as "permission" (cf. the very dif-

<hr />

[22] Cf. the article mentioned in note 14 (3) (especially the final section II, 2bβ).

ferent view, also in Luke: 22:35–38). For him, the command of Jesus only has *intentional* binding force—that is, with regard to the spirit behind it. In 1 Corinthians 7:10, 25 (40), he recommends that the ban on the "putting asunder" of married people (Mk 10:11f. parr) be observed at least in some *approximate* manner—at any rate not involving remarriage; no doubt this is to cater to cases where a separation has already occurred. In 1 Corinthians 7:12–16 Paul concedes, in spite of Mark 10:11f., that spouses may separate if the unbelieving husband insists; that is, he recommends that the command be followed approximately, as the situation demands. Matthew does the same, though in a different way: he remolds Jesus' ethical challenge into a legal community precept and, with his "except for unchastity" provision (Mt 5:32, 19:9), seems to be making concessions at the juridical level. (The exegete has no means at his disposal to decide whether these examples illustrate the existence of total authority in the apostolic age or in the postapostolic Church—that is, on the part of individual Christians.)

II

The Normative Character of Apostolic and Primitive Christian Values and Injunctions

The New Testament writings' claim to binding validity, quite apart from the conduct and words of Jesus, rests on the fact that they record the conduct and words of the apostles and other primitive Christian pneumatics, as well as the manner of life and tradition of the communities at the Church's inception. This "incipient Church" is normative (see the previous discussion) in that she was still being built up and stamped, in a special way, by the Spirit of the risen Lord. This must be emphasized, even though it must not be forgotten that "the Spirit of truth" will guide the disciples "into all the truth" (Jn 16:13)—which must apply in a particular manner to moral understanding.

Ultimately the binding quality of the apostolic tradition springs from the fact that it is this tradition that has "received Christ Jesus the Lord" (Col 2:6) and his mode of life—not only in terms of words, but in terms of life (thus 1 Th 2:13; 1 Cor 15:2 passim)—and hands it on.[23] It is here that people "learn Christ" (Eph 4:20f.). At the same time, the

[23] Cf. 1 Th 1:6; Phil 2:6–11; 3:18; Rom 15:1–5.

apostolic teaching and tradition in the communities, particularly in the "developing Church", is sustained by the Spirit of the exalted Lord (cf. 2 Cor 3:1–18).[24] The Kyrios manifests himself whenever he is preached (2 Cor 4:5f. passim); he is "near" in his word (cf. Rom 10:5–8a).

It was particularly, then, in the conduct (cf. 1 Th 2:11f.; 1 Cor 4:14ff. passim) and the teaching of the *apostles* that "the glory of Christ" (2 Cor 4:4) shone forth, working and speaking through them (2 Cor 3:1ff.; Rom 15:18), so that their word could become "the word of God" (1 Th 2:13). Paul admonishes "on behalf of Christ" (2 Cor 5:20), he "exhorts" (1 Th 4:10f.; 1 Cor 11:17), "rules" (1 Cor 7:17) "in the same way as the Lord" (1 Cor 9:14), because he "teaches [his] ways in Christ" (1 Cor 4:17). In the New Testament, the apostles are sometimes put together with other pneumatics, but they are always emphatically given first place (cf. 1 Cor 12:28f.; Eph 4:11). Thus too, later, the Pseudepigrapha—containing both apostolic and apocryphal tradition—will claim apostolic authority.

The theology of the Letter to the Ephesians closely links *prophets* with apostles as recipients of revelation (Eph 3:5; cf. Eph 3:3), as founders (cf. Eph 2:20) of the "growing Church". This juxta-

[24] Cf. more detail in the article mentioned in note 14 (3).

position is reproduced by ancient tradition (cf. 1 Cor 12:28f.; Eph 4:11). At the Church's inception this charism of prophecy existed side by side with the apostolic office, and to a heightened degree (cf. 1 Th 5:20; 1 Cor 12:10 passim); this universally normative quality was a feature of the founding era together with the charism of *receiving revelation* (1 Cor 14:6, 26; 1 Cor 14:30; 2 Cor 12:1; Eph 1:17).

Primitive Christian lists of charisms also mention the gift of *wisdom* (1 Cor 12:8; Eph 1:17; 1 Cor 2:6f. passim) and of *gnosis* (1 Cor 12:8; 13:8 passim), and also the ability to *instruct* one another (Rom 15:14 passim). The ministry of *teaching* (1 Cor 14:6, 26; cf. 12:28; Rom 12:7 passim) is rooted in these charisms. Thus, the values and precepts of the primitive Church are by no means determined solely by the gifts of the "apostles and prophets" (cf. 1 Cor 12:28ff.; Rom 12:6f.); beside them, more or less institutionalized, are the *teachers* (cf. 1 Cor 12:28; Gal 1:12; 6:6) and later the "pastors and teachers" (Eph 4:11). It is always clear, however, that they can only "teach" those who are themselves *taught by God* (1 Th 4:9; cf. Jer 31:34). All these charisms played their part in forming the community traditions; the communities' experience and teaching ultimately became a "standard of teaching" (Rom 6:17b), catechetical *logoi* (cf. Lk 1:4; 1 Tim 1:15; 3:1 passim). We must note that various primitive Christian values and injunctions differ a great deal, in form and content, with regard to their claims to be normative and their binding character. To a large extent their aims are practical and pastoral. In coming to an assessment of the binding moral implications of the primitive Christian paradosis as we find it in the New Testament, we would do well to distinguish (1) the theo-logically/eschato-logically oriented values and precepts, which describe appropriate conduct in the presence of the God who, in Christ, reveals himself eschatologically and brings about man's salvation, and (2) "particular" values and precepts referring to various areas of the world and of life.[25] The question as to their normative character must be put differently in each case.

[25] We are deliberately avoiding the increasingly widespread division into "transcendental" and "categorial" precepts lest the impression be given that a particular philosophy is being imported into the discussion. We do not speak of "formal" and "material" precepts, since even particular counsels and demands can remain general—and in this sense "formal". So too we do not talk in terms of a "salvation ethos" and a "world ethos", for all worldly activity has a significance for salvation.

1. The Theo-logically/Eschato-logically Oriented Values and Precepts

In the New Testament writings, moral exhortation (in terms both of intensity and frequency) concentrates on the values and precepts (mostly general and nonspecific in character) that call for a total, loving self-surrender in response to the eschatological love of God in Christ.[26] *They are seen as summed up in the twofold command (cf. Mk 12:28–34 parr) of love of God (i.e., of Christ) and, intimately connected with it, love of neighbor. Conduct, if it is to be appropriate to the given reality and to the particular situation—that is, if it is to do justice to the eschatological "hour" and the eschatological love of God, the saving work of Christ and the believer's baptismal character—must be situated at the intersection of this vertical love and its horizontal response.*

To attempt to deny the universal validity of the (general) admonitions and imperatives found in

[26] In New Testament terms, of course, the theo-logical and eschato-logical orientations and motivations can only be conceived as interpenetrating, with identical centers of gravity. However, once this is clearly understood, they can be discussed separately to illustrate something that applies to the majority of New Testament precepts; namely, that in, with and under the "eschatological" ethical factors there are also "theological" ones. These latter are not merely functional; ultimately, they have a personal, ontic foundation.

the New Testament writings would be to relativize the New Testament message of salvation, which is rooted in moral exhortation. For it sees the eschaton as having broken into world history, irrevocably, in the Incarnation (cf. Jn 1:14f.) and in the "once and for all" of Jesus' death (cf. Rom 6:10; Heb 7:27; 9:12; 10:10). This eschatological manifestation of God's love both elicits and demands a loving response on man's part.

a. A great number of the New Testament admonitions and imperatives summon us to respond lovingly and with faith to the advent of eschatological salvation— *in the saving work of Christ and in our own baptism— by acting in a way appropriate to the given reality and the particular situation. Other texts urge us to cultivate hope as we allow the* nearness of the Kingdom—*that is,* the parousia—*to make us ready and vigilant.*

As we have seen in the preaching of Jesus, moral exhortation was based more on the appearance of the eschaton as shown by God's saving action in Jesus (cf. Lk 11:20; Mt 18:23–24; Lk 7:36–47) than on the proximity of the end. This is equally true of Paul, John and the later New Testament writers. It is primarily the anamnesis of Christ's saving work (cf. Phil 2:6ff.; 1 Cor 14:7f., 15; 2 Cor 8:9; Rom 12:1) and the recalling of one's personal baptism (cf. Rom 6:1–23; 2 Cor 6:14–7:1; Col 3:1ff.; cf. 1 Pet 1:3–4, 11) that provide the foundation and motivation for the moral imperative.

b. Love is the soul of all theo-logically/eschato-logically oriented exhortations and imperatives, a love that responds both vertically and horizontally to the experience of God's eschatological love, or rather, that structures everything in an "incarnational" manner, seeing God in one's neighbor and one's neighbor in God.

The central demand of the New Testament, in whatever garb it is presented, is the demand for total self-giving that follows from the love of Christ or of God. This is the ultimate commandment and is absolutely binding.

Ultimately, Jesus' incomparably radical theocentrism draws its motivation from the experience of the absolute goodness and absolute Lordship of God, both of which are made manifest in the incipient eschaton. In the post–Easter perspective, God's saving word that demands a response becomes especially clear in the death and resurrection of Jesus; it is not fortuitous that, in Paul, the call to love Christ (cf. 1 Cor 16:22; 2 Cor 5:14ff.; Rom 14:7ff.; cf. Eph 6:24) takes up more space than the call to love God (which only occurs explicitly in 1 Cor 2:9; 8:3; Rom 8:28). The summons to total self-giving, presented variously in the different

33

New Testament writings, is the horizon for all New Testament ethical demands.

In the New Testament, however, we very frequently meet with the command to love *our neighbor, our* brother. *This too is put variously in the different writings. Often it is related to the attitude of the Son of God (e.g., Phil 2:6ff.; 2 Cor 8:9 passim) or the love of God (cf. 1 Jn 4:11 passim). Thus, the command of love, claiming to be "the law of Christ" (Gal 6:2), the "new commandment" (Jn 13:34; 15:12; 1 Jn 2:7f.), binds us absolutely to fulfill it, at least insofar as it remains general and nonspecific.*

For the commandment of love "sums up" (Rom 13:8ff.) and "fulfills" (Gal 5:14) the Old Testament law; that is, the latter is "concentrated" in it and "intentionalized" (cf. Mt 7:12; 22:40) toward it. Thus its validity is as real and unconditional as that of the Torah of Moses, as we can see from the very terms "the law of Christ" and "the new commandment"—albeit the concept of law here is used in a paradoxical sense that stretches it to the breaking point and shatters it. (In the same way the conduct of the "Son"—i.e., his self-abasing and self-emptying love—goes beyond the laws of what is "human".)

34

2. The Particular Values and Precepts

Within the context of the foregoing theo-logical/eschato-logical values and precepts, the New Testament contains other values and precepts that refer to individual and specific areas of life in the world; that is, to specific actions. In a certain sense—although in a very different manner—these too claim an abiding validity. It seems wise to distinguish the mass of New Testament "spiritual precepts" from those that are "ethical" in the narrower sense (see the following discussion), even though the distinction between them is not always a sharp one.

In the case of particular values and precepts, judgment must be "mixed", albeit in varying degrees. Even where general values and attitudes are concerned, our grasp of the relevant general areas of the world and of life may be inadequate—out of proportion, partly understressed, partly overstressed—and this and other factors may mean that our judgment will be bounded by our time and our milieu. But where concrete values and precepts are concerned, it is not only that the value itself can be misjudged; as well as this, in formulating operative norms of action or in giving directions for individual concrete acts, the concrete state of affairs and the historical situation can be misconceived. This means that, where particular values and precepts are concerned, the demands put forward by the biblical writers can be influenced by time-bound values and an inadequate estimate of the world and of life (that is, of concrete matters of fact and situation), with the result that, in changed historical circumstances, there must be different evaluations and judgments. In cases such as this it is only by analogy—that is, approximately—that we can speak of a "permanent" normative character. What is subject to the norm is the underlying intention; the concrete application will involve adaptation. The exegete cannot decide in isolation how these norms are to be applied in all particular areas, since it is only through dialogue involving other theological and nontheological disciplines that an assessment of the actual state of affairs can be reached.

a. It must be very evident that a large proportion of the particular values and precepts that claim to govern the life of the community are spiritual *in kind. In the New Testament, for instance, such values and precepts constitute a "fraternal community ethic". Quite clearly, exhortations to joy (Phil 3:1; Rom 12:15), to prayer without ceasing (cf. 1 Th 5:17), to thanksgiving (1 Th 5:18; Col 3:17), to "foolishness" (1 Cor 3:18ff.), to indifference (1 Cor 7:29ff.) are permanent Christian goals and injunctions; they are "fruits of the Spirit" (cf. Gal 5:22). Others are by way of "counsel" (e.g.,*

1 Cor 7:17, 27ff.). All are particular forms of the basic exhortation, which is "Be filled with the Spirit" (Eph 5:18) and "walk by the Spirit" (Gal 5:16). In the New Testament these "spiritual precepts" are strongly emphasized. Where they are formulated in general terms, their permanent normative character can scarcely be questioned; their significance cannot be played down in favor of a positivistic secular spirituality and an ethics of worldly involvement.

It is a fact that many of these spiritual precepts are formulated in a highly concrete manner, which means that, in the twentieth century situation of the Christian community, they cannot be adhered to as presented (cf. chapters 7–17 of 1 Cor; Col 3:16; Eph 5:19). We must not be too quick to characterize them as paradigms and as models of conduct; rather, we should ask seriously whether they can still be followed today in an analogous or approximate manner, suitably adapted and at the level of intention.

b. So far as the ethical exhortations and precepts (in the narrower sense) are concerned, we can first of all distinguish the large number of social attitudes and practices, which are the concrete historical embodiment of the love of neighbor, from other, particular attitudes and practices, though here again it is impossible to make an absolutely clear distinction.

37

Love of neighbor can be embodied in social attitudes and practices; these are as varied as everyday human intercourse dictates: love is patient and kind, love bears all things, believes all things, hopes all things, endures all things; love is not jealous or boastful; it is not arrogant or rude. Love does not insist on its own way; it is not irritable or resentful; it does not rejoice at wrong, but rejoices in the right (cf. 1 Cor 13:4–7; cf. also 1 Th 5:14f.; Col 3:12f. passim). Since these and similar "social" attitudes have a special closeness to the command of love (see the previous discussion), and since the Christian has been baptized into a Christian brotherhood and is essentially a community being who will always have to live together with imperfect human beings, these demands lose nothing of their significance and binding character.

Wherever the commandment of love is "embodied" in practical norms of conduct and particular concrete prescriptions, we have to establish whether and in what way the fundamental demand is colored, not only by time-bound values, but also by particular historical conditions. Thus, we shall be able to see how, in a changed situation, the command can be followed analogously, by way of approximation, suitably adapted and at the level of intention. We cannot ignore the fact that many of the Pauline exhortations are thoroughly shaped by the special situation of the embryonic Church;

more explicitly, they are rooted in the prevailing conditions of the communities of the time[27] and show the influence of time-bound values.[28] A moral-theological hermeneutics must ask how their claim to be valid today might be formulated.

In the New Testament writings, besides the "social" attitudes and practices referred to, we also find ethical values and precepts that are concerned primarily with other particular spheres of life, *although these too— more or less—are situated in the context of the demands made by love. As regards ethical values and practical norms (i.e., concrete prescriptions), if we are to gain an understanding of their binding character, we must take account of the way in which they draw their motivation from theo-logical and eschato-logical considerations, from the demands of love or from fundamental requirements of a generally ethical kind. We must also note their* sitz im leben *in the life of the communities. We shall have to face the fact that many of the practical ethical values and precepts relating to particular areas of life are colored and overlaid, and hence relativized, by time-bound values and judgments of fact. Even if only* one *such instance can be demonstrated in the New Testament—as seems possible (see the following discussion)—it will be a vindication of the fundamental right of hermeneutics to*

[27] Cf. 1 Cor 4:1–13; 10:23–11:1; Rom 14:1–15, 6.
[28] 1 Cor 7:1–7; Col 3:19; cf. Eph 5:25–30; Col 3:22f.; Philemon.

question the basis on which New Testament values and precepts rest.

The warnings against idolatry (Gal 5:20 passim) and also against the major vices of paganism[29]—*impurity* (1 Th 4:3ff. passim) and *deceit* (1 Th 4:6)—have a strong claim to be observed, since here, in the baptismal exhortation (cf. Eph 4:17–24!), the baptized are being given basic moral instruction. However, when the New Testament writers see *the wife as subject to the husband* (cf. 1 Cor 11:2–16; 14:33–36 passim), a view which we can understand as being of its time, we feel that the Holy Spirit has led Christians today, along with the contemporary environment, into a deeper understanding of the moral obligations of personal relationships than that enjoyed by the primitive Christian generation. The injunction to submit to *state authority* (Rom 13:1–7) must be taken together with 1 Corinthians 6:1–7, where Paul himself shows his own reserve toward state authority, and 1 Corinthians 2:8, where he acknowledges that there can be unjust state authority. (In any case, such precepts must be seen in the context of the whole of the New Testament; cf., e.g., Lk 4:5ff., Rev passim.) What-

[29] Cf. the stereotyped association of licentiousness and deceit in 1 Th 4:3–8; 1 Cor 5:9ff.; Col 3:5; cf. Eph 4:19; 5:3ff.—clearly a theme in baptismal instruction (cf. Eph 4:17–24).

ever the cultural context may be, in 1 Corinthians 11:2–16 Paul is ultimately concerned (cf. v. 16) simply to have a community custom ("practice") observed; namely, that the *woman* shall be *veiled* when praying and shall not *speak in prophecy*. It would be totally inappropriate to hold it against Paul that he does not actively campaign against a society that maintains *slavery* (cf. 1 Cor 7:21–24; Col 3:22–4:1; Philemon), although objectively, it must be recognized that his moral judgment at this point is impaired—for historically determined and quite understandable reasons. The one-sided way in which the Matthaean account of the Lord's words disqualifies the Pharisees (e.g., Mt 23) and later tradition treats Jews (e.g., 1 Th 2:15f.), pagans (e.g., Rom 1:26–32) or heretics (2 Pet 2:10–22; Jude 8–16 passim) cannot be regarded as a model in every respect and for all time.

Summary

Most, by far, of the New Testament values and precepts are designed to elicit an appropriate attitude toward the love of God made manifest eschatologically in Christ. Thus, they open up a theo-logical and eschato-logical horizon and call for an answering love of God (of Christ) and of the neighbor. This applies not only to those demands in the New Testament that claim to be absolutely binding, arising from the conduct and the words of Jesus (I), but also to the majority of apostolic instructions and those originating in the primitive Church (II, 1). Values and precepts of this kind, though in different ways, are absolute in their intention and in the validity to which they lay claim. Even the values and precepts that are concerned with particular areas of life (II, 2) share to a large extent in that same horizon, especially where it is a case of "spiritual" injunctions of a general kind (II, 2a). We have seen that, even in the relatively narrow area of ethical values and precepts in the more restricted sense (II, 2b), the "social" precepts, insofar as they remain general and are related to the commandment of love, as well as the fundamental requirements of baptismal instruction, formulated in general terms, have a permanently binding character that is beyond question. It is otherwise with a number of practical norms of conduct and particular injunctions which, though "spiritual" can clearly be seen to be time bound (cf. II, 2a), and also in the case of individual "ethical" precepts in the narrower sense (cf. II, 2b), where the New Testament judgments and exhortations must submit to scrutiny.

Thus, the foregoing outline lends no support to the generalization that all New Testament values and precepts are limited in validity to their own time, at least so far as the particular or the practical norms of conduct are concerned. It is only proper to speak of their "paradigmatic" character, of their being "models of conduct", where their literary form can be shown exegetically to substantiate such a claim. In other cases we do more justice to the New Testament precepts by examining how they may be followed in an approximate sense, analogously, through adaptation and in terms of underlying intention.

Here and there among the particular New Testament values and precepts, however, there are time-bound judgments of value and of fact, and they show that the Holy Spirit has deepened moral sensitivity through the course of the Church's history and the history of mankind. Consequently, there is a basis for a moral-theological hermeneutics with regard to such moral values and precepts in the New Testament writings. Yet, if we take the significance of Holy Scripture seriously (cf. our introductory remarks), this hermeneutics will not be able to proceed either in a purely biblicist or a purely rationalist manner in seeking out the *criteria moralitatis* and the *criteria theologiae moralis*. It will have to reach its understanding through "encounter"—in the ever-fresh confrontation of modern critical knowledge with the moral insights of Holy Scripture. It remains true that it is only by listening to the Word of God (*Dei Verbum audiens*[30]) that modern critical knowledge can be safely interpreted as "signs of the times" in which the Spirit of God is at work. Yet this is what must take place in the community of the People of God[31]—in the unity of the *sensus fidelium* and the magisterium assisted by the whole of theology. The exegete cannot decide questions of moral-theological hermeneutics on his own; the foregoing "propositions" simply aim to highlight a number of aspects with which the exegete is faced.

[30] Cf. *Dei Verbum* 1.
[31] Cf. the article mentioned in note 14 (1).

JOSEPH RATZINGER

The Church's Teaching
Authority—Faith—Morals

An outline of the problem

The crisis of faith that is increasingly making itself felt by Christian people is revealing itself with increasing clarity as a crisis regarding awareness of fundamental values of human life. It is nourished by the moral crisis of mankind, and at the same time it intensifies this crisis. Trying to come to an appreciation of the whole sweep of current discussion on this question, however, one meets with notions that, though strangely contrary, are all the same closely connected. On the one hand, particularly since the formation of the World Council of Churches in Uppsala, there is an increasingly clear trend to view Christianity primarily not as "orthodoxy" but as "orthopraxy". Many factors have contributed to this trend. There is, for instance, the question of racial equality in America, which has had a serious influence on Christianity there, since it is evident that the existence of a common confession of faith has done nothing to break down the wall of division. Thus, the concrete value of the confession of faith has become questionable, as it has no power to arouse love, which is the root of the gospel. Here we see a practical question becoming the touchstone for the truth of doctrine, a test case for the Christian position; where "orthopraxy" is so scandalously lacking, "orthodoxy" becomes questionable.

Another factor in the trend toward "praxis" lies in the various strands of "political theology", which are in turn variously motivated. They are all deeply affected by the questions raised by Marxism. Here, the concept of "truth" is itself under suspicion, if not devoid of content. To that extent, this mode of thought is one with the sentiment that gives rise to positivism. Truth is felt to be unattainable, and the insistence on truth is regarded as the ploy of interest groups seeking to confirm their position. According to this view, only praxis can decide the value or worthlessness of theories. If Christianity, therefore, wishes to contribute to a better world, it must come up with a better praxis—not seeking truth as a theory, but producing it as a reality. Here, the demand that Christianity must become an "orthopraxy" of common action toward a more human future, leaving orthodoxy behind as something unfruitful or even positively harmful, is far more radical than in the purely pragmatic positions mentioned earlier. At the same time it is clear that the two approaches tend to combine operations and reinforce one another. Neither of them has much space left for a teaching authority, although, if these views were carried through consistently, it would inevitably reemerge in a different form. But a teaching authority that would formulate an already-given truth concerning man's authentic praxis and that would

48

measure man's performance against this truth would be banished to the negative side of reality as a hindrance to creative and forward-looking praxis. It would be regarded as a symptom of particular interests hiding behind the slogan of "orthodoxy" and opposing the onward march of the history of freedom. On the other hand, it is admitted that praxis needs reflection and tactics resulting from reflection; so the linking of Marxist praxis to the Party's "teaching authority" is completely logical.

At the opposite end from the view that would define and realize Christianity in terms of ortho-praxy there is a position (often—unaccountably—embracing the former) that affirms that there is no such thing as a specifically Christian morality and that Christianity must take its norms of conduct from the anthropological insights of its time. Faith does not supply any independent source of moral norms, but points insistently to the future. Nothing that is not ratified by the future can be maintained by faith. This view is substantiated by indicating that, even in its historical roots, faith does not develop a morality of its own, but adopts the practical reason of contemporary men and women.[1]

---

[1] Thus, H. Küng, *On Being a Christian* (London, 1977), 542: "The distinguishing feature even of the Old Testament ethos did not consist in the individual precepts or prohibitions, but in the Yahweh faith. . . . The directives of the 'second

This can already be seen in the Old Testament, where there is a continual change going on in values from the time of the patriarchs to the Wisdom literature, determined by the encounter with the developing moral ideas of the surrounding cultures. There is no moral proposition found exclusively in the Old Testament that can be regarded solely as the fruit of faith in Yahweh; in moral matters everything is taken over from elsewhere. This applies to the New Testament as well: the lists of virtues and vices in the apostolic Letters reflect the Stoic ethos and thus represent the adoption of what was currently reason's guide for human conduct. Consequently it is not their content, but their structure, that is significant, in that they

---

tablet' . . . have numerous analogies in the Near East. . . . These fundamental minimal requirements then are not specifically Israelite. . . . All that is specifically Israelite is the fact that these requirements are subordinated to the authority of Yahweh, the God of the Covenant. . . ." In reply to this we must ask: Did Israel's idea of God, then, arise without any borrowing, without any parallels in its environment? Is it not the case that, in the East, as elsewhere, ethical and legal demands are associated with the authority of the people's particular deity? Similar questions raise their heads when we find Küng speaking of the New Testament thus: "The ethical requirements of the New Testament . . . did not fall from heaven either in content or in form" (543). Does he imply that the rest of the New Testament *did* fall from heaven? Clearly, there can be no argument along these lines.

point to reason as the only source of moral norms. We need hardly say that, here too, there is no place for a Church teaching authority in moral matters; for to set up detailed norms of conduct on the basis of the tradition of faith would be to act on the misconception that the statements of the Bible have an abiding validity in terms of content, whereas, according to this view, they only point to the particular stage reached at the time by rational human understanding.

Both approaches clearly raise fundamental problems regarding the nature of the Christian position that cannot be fully dealt with in a few pages. In the first case, where Christianity is interpreted as "orthopraxy" not only pragmatically but in principle, the basic issue is the question of truth, of what is reality. Ultimately, the question of being is inextricably involved with the first article of faith, even if, in particular instances, people are not always aware of it, and the positions adopted are rarely carried through in absolute consistency. At first sight, the second case seems to revolve around a single historical problem; that is, the historical origin of certain biblical statements. But if we look closer we find that it rests on a more fundamental problem; namely, the question of how what is specifically Christian can be defined vis-à-vis the changing historical forms it adopts. It also involves the problem of how faith communicates with reason, with universally human aspects, and ultimately the question of reason's sphere of action and limitations in matters of faith.[2]

An initial response

Let us begin with the most immediate aspect, which is simplest to deal with, and thus come to grips with the problem of the historical origins of

[2] This question is carefully discussed—though in pursuing quite a different course—in B. Schüller, "Die Bedeutung des natürlichen Sittengesetzes für den Christen", in G. Teichtweier and W. Dreier, *Herausforderung und Kritik der Moraltheologie* (Würzburg, 1971), 105–130. The following quotation can be regarded as a summary of the synthesis he attempts: "In view of the fact that all ethical demands are in principle accessible to rational insight, the ethical message of the New Testament must be seen as a communication of ethical insight in a Socratic manner" (118). Here everything depends on how one interprets his "in principle accessible to rational insight", and what is meant by "Socratic". I cannot shake off the impression that Schüller is using the concept of "reason" all too blithely, as if it were unproblematic. See, e.g. p. 111: "Romans 1 suggests that man is aware of himself as a moral being. This being so, reason can appreciate the validity of the commandment to love God and one's neighbor." This basic position is certainly fundamental; yet what is gravely lacking is the realistic context of experience by which Paul explicates and qualifies it.

biblical utterances on moral issues. First of all there is a general question of methodology, for it is quite simply wrong to say that things inherited from elsewhere can never attain separate and distinctive existence. Our own life tells us this; the theological affirmation "What have you that you did not receive?" can be demonstrated even at a purely human level. We know it, too, from the whole history of civilization: the greatness of a civilization is seen in its ability to communicate, its ability to give and receive, but in particular to receive, to assimilate elements into itself. The originality of Christianity does not consist in the number of propositions for which no parallel can be found elsewhere (if there *are* such propositions, which is highly questionable). It is impossible to distill out what is specifically Christian by excluding everything that has come about through contact with other milieux. Christianity's originality consists rather in the new total form into which human searching and striving have been forged under the guidance of faith in the God of Abraham, the God of Jesus Christ. The fact that the Bible's moral pronouncements can be traced to other cultures or to philosophical thought in no way implies that morality is a function of mere reason—this is a premature conclusion we should not allow to pass unchallenged any longer. What is important is not that such utterances can be found elsewhere, but the particular position they have or do not have in the spiritual edifice of Christianity. This is what we must now examine.

Let us begin with an absolutely simple observation. Historically speaking, it is incorrect to say that biblical faith simply adopted the morality of the surrounding world—that is, the particular stage of rational moral awareness that had been reached at the time—for there was no "surrounding world", no "environment" as such, nor was there a single "morality" that could have been adopted. What we find is that, guided by Israel's perception of Yahweh, an often highly dramatic struggle took place between those elements of the surrounding legal and moral tradition that could be assimilated by Israel and those that Israel was bound to reject. In the final analysis this is what the prophets are fighting for. Thus Nathan forbids David to adopt the manner of an absolute oriental potentate who would take someone else's wife if he so desired. Thus Elijah, in championing Naboth's rights, is defending the rights of the nation, guaranteed by the God of Israel, against royal absolutism. So too Amos, in fighting for the rights of the hired laborer, and of all dependent people, is vindicating the vision of the God of Israel. It is always the same story. Similarly, the many-sided struggle between Yahweh and Baal cannot be reduced to a merely "dogmatic" question; what is at stake here is the indivisible unity of faith and life. Deciding for or against the one God or the many gods is always a life decision.

Three examples of the interrelation of faith and morals

a. The Ten Commandments

We come now to a more detailed discussion, which will be clarified somewhat by three characteristic examples. First let us consider the Ten Commandments (Ex 20:1–17; Dt 5:6–21), one of the central formulations of Yahweh's will for Israel, which has always been a formative influence on the ethos of Israel and of the Church. No doubt it can be shown that there are precedents, both in Egyptian lists of transgressions to be avoided and in the interrogations of Babylonian exorcisms. Even the introductory formula "I am the Lord your God" is not entirely new. Yet it imparts a new face to the "Ten Words", linking them to the God of the Covenant and his Covenant will. The "Ten Words" show in practical terms what it means to believe in Yahweh, to accept the covenant with Yahweh. At the same time they define the figure of God himself, whose nature is manifested through them. This situates the Ten Commandments in the context of God's decisive self-revelation in Exodus 3, for there too God's self-portrayal is expressed in practical terms by setting forth his moral will: he has heard the groanings of the oppressed and has come to liberate them. The introduction to the Ten Commandments, both in the Exodus 20 version and in the form in Deuteronomy, links up with this revelation: Yahweh introduces himself as the God who brought Israel out of Egypt, out of the house of bondage. In other words, for Israel, the Ten Commandments are part of the concept of God. They are not supplementary to faith, to the Covenant; they show who this God is, with whom Israel stands in a covenant relationship.[3]

Connected with this is the concept of the "holy" as it has developed in the religion of the Bible. In the history of religions in general, "holiness" is simply the divinity's total otherness, the specific atmosphere of divinity, yielding particular rules for encountering it. Initially, Israel is no different in this regard, as many passages show. Since Yahweh, however, reveals what is special about him, his complete otherness, through the "Ten Words", it becomes clear (and the prophets increasingly call it to mind) that Yahweh's total otherness, his "holiness", is a moral dimension; to

[3] Cf. H. Cazelles, "Dekalog", in H. Haag, *Bibel-Lexikon* (Benziger, 1968), 319–323 (lit.); G. von Rad, *Old Testament Theology* I (London, 1975), 190ff.

it corresponds man's moral action in accord with the "Ten Words". In the ancient layers of tradition to which the Ten Commandments belong, the concept of the "holy" as the specific category of the divine has already coalesced with the concept of the "moral"; that is what is new and unique about this God and his holiness. It is also what imparts a new status to the category of the "moral", and it provides criteria of selection in the debate with the ethos of the nations, eventually attaining the heights of that concept of holiness in the Old Testament that anticipates Jesus' own picture of God: "I will not execute my fierce anger . . . for I am God and not man, the Holy One in your midst . . ." (Hos 11:9). "Now there can be no doubt that it is the proclamation of the Decalogue over her which puts Israel's election into effect", as Gerhard von Rad formulates it in his *Old Testament Theology*; he also illustrates this connection by showing its effects upon liturgical life.[4] This by no means implies that the Ten Commandments were understood, right from the outset, in the fullness of their significance; nor that the mere word alone communicates fundamental moral understanding in a definitive form: on the contrary, the history of interpretation, from the earliest strands of tradition right up to the re-

[4] G. von Rad, *Old Testament Theology* I, 192.

casting of the Ten Commandments in the Sermon on the Mount, shows that this word could (and was bound to) ignite an ever-deeper understanding of the will of God, and hence of God and of man. On the other hand, as we have said, the fact that particular elements of the Ten Commandments can be traced to non-Israelite origins tells us nothing about whether or not they can be separated off from the core of covenant faith. Such a view can only be maintained if one assumes that there is no analogy between the nations' reason and God's revelation, and that the two phenomena confront each other in a pure paradox; that is, if one has a particular concept of the relationship between revelation and reason, a concept that is not verified by the biblical texts, but rather is falsified by them.

b. The name "Christian"

Let us take another example, this time from the early Christian period; namely, the significance of the words "Christian" and "Christianity" in the Church's initial development.[5] Here again, as with

[5] Cf. esp. E. Peterson, "Christianus", in his *Frühkirche, Judentum und Gnosis* (Freiburg, 1959), 64–87. I have received valuable pointers on this issue from the thesis submitted to the University of Regensburg in 1974 by K. Bommes: *Das Verständnis des Martyriums bei Ignatius von Antiochien*.

the Ten Commandments in Israel, it is the central core itself that is speaking. From Acts 11:26 we know that this name was first applied in Antioch to the community of believers. Though the occasion that gave rise to this epithet is lost to us, and its original signification is disputed (and will remain so, given the sources available to us), there was clearly something ironic about it in the beginning. Moreover, in Roman law it denoted a punishable offence: the *christiani* were members of Christ's band of conspirators; from the time of Hadrian, therefore, bearing the name "Christian" was a crime. Peterson has shown that the charges laid against Christians—in Suetonius and Tacitus, for instance—are an integral part of political propaganda "against real or alleged conspirators".[6] Yet in Ignatius of Antioch we already find Christians applying this dangerous title to themselves; indeed, they are proud to bear it and to prove worthy of it. What does it mean, therefore, when people deliberately adopt a term of abuse, a criminal title?

The answer is twofold. First of all we find in Ignatius a strongly marked theology of martyrdom, which leads to the adoption of the word that itself involves martyrdom. Fellowship with Jesus Christ, which faith is, signifies to the eyes of the world a participation in a conspiracy punishable by death.

[6] Peterson, 80.

The Bishop of Antioch realizes that this "external" verdict somehow or other actually hits upon a central truth, although the way in which it is true is internal: fellowship with Jesus *is in fact* a participation in his death, and thus (only thus) in his life.[7] The idea that Christians are united in a conspiracy with Christ is correct insofar as Christians do not merely adopt a theory about Jesus, but enter into his way of living and dying and make it their own. "Since we have become his disciples, we must learn how to live in accordance with Christianity."[8] In this sense, so far as the Syrian martyr-bishop is concerned, Christianity is most definitely an "orthopraxy"—it is a realization of Jesus Christ's manner of life. But what form does that take? To answer this question we must go one step farther. For the pagan, the word *christianus* meant a conspirator, represented in the stereotypes of political propaganda as a person characterized by evil *flagitia* (crimes); in particular, by "hatred against the human race" and by *stuprum* (licentiousness).[9] In response Ignatius uses a play on words that came to have a long history in Christian apologetics. In Greek phonetics, the word *chrestos* ("good"), was, and is, pronounced *christos*. Ignatius seizes on this association when he prefaces the words "we must

[7] *Magn.* 5:1f.
[8] *Magn.* 10:1.
[9] Peterson, 77ff.

60

learn how to live in accordance with Christianity [*christianismos*]" with the admonition "let us not be unfeeling toward his goodness [*chrestotes*, pronounced *christotes*]."[10] The conspiracy of the *Christos* is a conspiracy of those who are *chrestos*, a conspiracy of goodness. Thus Tertullian, a hundred years later, will assert that "the word Christ comes from the word for goodness."[11] Here, the link we found in the Ten Commandments between the concept of God and the moral idea is repeated at a most sublime and exacting level in the Christian context: the name "Christian" implies fellowship with Christ, and hence the readiness to take upon oneself martyrdom in the cause of goodness. Christianity is a conspiracy to promote the good; the theological and moral aspects are fused inseparably, both in the word itself and deeper, in the basic concept of what Christian reality is.[12]

[10] *Magn.* 10:1.

[11] *Apol* III 5 (C Chr I 92); *Ad Nat* I 3, 8f. (C Chr I 14): *Christianum vero nomen . . . de unctione interpretatur. Etiam cum corrupte a vobis Chrestiani pronuntiamur . . . sic quoque de suavitate vel bonitate modulatum est.* Cf. Peterson, 85.

[12] Thus, doctrine and life are mutually interdependent in the Christian baptismal catechesis as in the baptismal rite, where the structure of affirmation and rejection combines the profession of faith with a moral confession (and vow). Not only is this unity basic to the whole patristic tradition from Justin (e.g., *Apol* I 61, 1: ὅσοι ἄν . . . πιστεύωσιν ἀληθῆ ταῦτα

c. The apostolic exhortation

Thus Ignatius and the early Christian theology that follows him stand foursquare on the foundation of apostolic preaching, which brings us to our third example. In Pauline preaching, in particular, there is an intimate connection between faith and "imitating" the apostle, who in turn "imitates" Jesus Christ. This is put especially clearly in 1 Thessalonians: "As you learned from us how you ought to live . . . do so more and more. For you know what instructions we gave you through the Lord Jesus" (1 Th 4:1ff.). This manner of life, this "walking" (AV) is part of the transmitted tradition; Paul's instruction does not come from just anywhere; it comes from the Lord Jesus. His subsequent remarks are loosely related to the Ten Commandments and apply them in a Christian sense to the particular situation of the Thessalonians.

. . . καὶ βιοῦν οὕτως δύνασθαι ὑπισχνῶνται to Basil (*De Spiritu Sancto* 15, 35f. PG 32, 130f., where the whole interpretation of the central baptismal action is dependent on it); it applies to the New Testament itself, where the moral exhortation in the Letters clearly points to baptismal catechesis and baptismal obligations. So the preaching of John the Baptist could be read as a Christian prebaptismal catechesis: cf. the interpretation of Lk 3:1–20 in H. Schürmann, *Das Lukasevangelium* I (Freiburg, 1969), 148–187.

Now it might be objected that what is at stake here is simply the formal intention toward the "good", which is no doubt characteristic of Christianity; but as to the question of what this goodness involves, this is something to be decided by reason and in the light of the times, not on the basis of internal theological sources. This seems to be suggested, for instance, by a text such as Philippians 4:8: "Finally, brethren, whatever is true, whatever is honorable, whatever is just, whatever is pure, whatever is lovely, whatever is gracious, if there is any excellence, if there is anything worthy of praise, think about these things." What we have here, it might be said, are current notions of popular philosophy; accepted notions of what is good are being commended to Christians for their acceptance too. To this we could immediately reply that the passage goes on: "What you have learned and received and heard and seen in me, do" (4:9). We could point out that this is ultimately an interpretation of 2:5: "Have this mind among yourselves, which was in Christ Jesus"— which reveals the same connection between the attitude of Jesus (as the standard of behavior) and Christian existence that we met in Ignatius.

But we must probe a little deeper. No doubt it is correct that, here as elsewhere, Paul is referring to the moral awareness that conscience has awakened among the pagans, and that he identifies this awareness with the true law of God, according to the principles developed in Romans 2:15. This does not mean, however, that the kerygma shrinks to a nonspecific pointer to whatever contemporary reason regards as good. In the first place, there has never been this kind of "contemporary reason", nor will there be. Paul was confronted, not with a particular scholarly consensus on the subject of the "good" to be simply adopted, but with a maze of conflicting positions, in which Epicurus and Seneca are only two examples of the whole spectrum. The only way to proceed here was not to accept the given, but through resolute critical discernment. It was a case of the Christian faith making its new decisions on the basis of the Old Testament tradition and, in concrete terms, of the "mind of Christ"; from outside this was condemned as "conspiracy", whereas from inside it was proclaimed all the more insistently as the genuine "good". Second, it is not true to say that, for Paul, conscience and reason are variables, one thing today and something else tomorrow. Conscience is shown to be what it is precisely because it says the same thing that God proclaimed to the Jews in the word of the Covenant. Conscience, as such, uncovers what is constant and thus necessarily leads to the "mind of Christ". Paul's real view of things comes to light most clearly, perhaps, in the first chapter of Romans, where we find that same connection between moral issues and the concept of God that we saw to be characteristic of the Old Testament: a faulty concept of God leads to faulty moral behavior in the pagan world; returning to God in Jesus Christ is identical with a return to the manner of life of Jesus Christ. Paul had already put forward this view in 1 Thessalonians: the pagans' unholiness is connected with the fact that they do not know God; the will of God is for their "sanctification", and the gospel of grace understands this morally. Anyone who reads the Pauline letters carefully will see that the apostolic exhortation is not some moralizing appendix with a variable content, but a very practical setting forth of what faith means; thus, it is inseparable from faith's core. The apostle is in fact only following the pattern of Christ, who, in this central theme of his preaching, linked admission to the Kingdom of God and exclusion from it with fundamental moral decisions, which are consequences intimately related to the way God is conceived.[13]

[13] I have deliberately avoided becoming involved with the specialists' debate in current moral theology concerning "deontological" or merely "teleological" ethical norms. For a perceptive and thorough treatment, cf. B. Schüller, "Neuere Beiträge zum Thema 'Begründung sittlicher Normen' ", in J. Pfammatter and F. Furger, *Theologische Berichte* IV (Einsiedeln, 1974), 109–181. As far as the establishment of concepts and a methodically worked-out system are concerned,

Faith—morals—teaching authority

In mentioning the apostolic exhortation we have gone beyond the connection of faith and morals and raised the question of teaching authority, for the apostolic Letters are instances of the exercise of

any answer must be sought within the technical debate and cannot be prejudged on the basis of the preconceptual nature of the biblical facts. In spite of this necessary methodological limitation, there *are* pointers which, so far as I can see, have not been sufficiently taken account of up to now. In this context the "short formulas" produced by the "teleological norm" approach are clearly inadequate; e.g., "Intrinsically evil and thus absolutely to be avoided is every action which objectively—according to right reason—fails to do justice to concrete human reality" (J. Fuchs, "Der Absolutheitscharakter sittlicher Handlungsnormen", in *Testimonium Veritatis* (Frankfurt, 1971), 211–240. We would have to ask what is meant by "concrete human reality" and "right reason"; in propositions such as these, the expressions are only formal and ultimately say nothing, even if, like Schüller (173), one attempts to fill them with definite content in the sense of Kant's categorical imperative. Even if the problems of establishing concepts and of systematization are left open, we still need to ask whether, in the light of the clear and constant elements that manifest themselves in the course of the biblical history of faith and are fixed in baptismal catechesis, there is not an indispensable bedrock of "deontological" norms. As I have already indicated in note 2, I feel that the real problem here lies in the abstract neutrality of the concept of reason, operating without people being aware of it; further discussion would need to address itself particularly to this issue.

teaching authority. Here Paul is also putting forward "official" teaching about the moral form that faith takes; the same applies to the other New Testament letters, as well as the Gospels, which are full of moral instruction, and finally the Book of Revelation. Paul does not offer theories about what is human and reasonable; what he does is explicate the inner demands of grace, as H. Schlier has shown in his fine article on the uniqueness of Christian moral exhortation.[14] True, the apostle does not use expressed commands very often (1 Th 4:10f.), although he is aware that he has the authority to do so (2 Cor 8:8); he does not want to approach the Christian communities as the pedagogues of the ancient world treated their pupils, with threats and with force, but prefers to admonish them as a father within the Christian family. In doing so, he shows clearly that it is the mercy of God that is calling to them through his words. It is grace, it is God exhorting them through Paul's exhortation; it is not some supplementary variable added to the Gospel: it is clothed with the Lord's authority, even when it does not appear in the form of a command or of an official doctrinal decision.[15] The same thing is observable if we

[14] H. Schlier, *Besinnung auf das Neue Testament* (Freiburg, 1964), 340–357.
[15] Ibid., 341–344.

examine the central themes of his exhortation—the saving events in Christ himself; baptism; fellowship of the Body of Christ; the prospect of the Last Judgment. [16] There is a clearly drawn line between grace and the manner of life of those who do not know God; it is described as a turning away from licentiousness, covetousness, idolatry, envy and quarrelsomeness, and a turning toward obedience, patience, truth, freedom from anxiety and joy. The fundamental commandment of love expresses itself in these attitudes. [17]

What we observe in Paul is continued in the writings of those taught by the apostles; here the apostolic exhortation, as a normative tradition, is expounded as it applies to the particular situation. [18] This means that, so far as the New Testament is

[16] Ibid., 344–352. Paul here is just as much aware of the "teleological" aspect (the coming judgment and reward/ punishment) as of the "deontological" aspect (e.g., his argument from the implications of being a member of the Body of Christ).

[17] Ibid., 352ff., esp. 355.

[18] Ibid., 343: "The pupils of the apostles and the other Christians all exhort on the basis of the apostolic exhortation; they take it as a normative tradition and apply it to their particular situation." I regard this as a fundamental statement with respect to the permanent substantive basis of Christian ethics and its nature as a whole; i.e., the development of the apostolic exhortation as a normative tradition in the face of particular situations.

concerned, the Church's official teaching does not come to an end with the age of the apostles; it is a permanent gift to the Church. The Church remains apostolic in the postapostolic age in that the authentic followers of the apostles bear responsibility to see that the Church abides in the teaching of the apostles. Luke stresses this in the crisis of transition, when he portrays the primitive Jerusalem community with its "remaining in the teaching of the apostles" (Acts 2:42) as the standard form of the Church for all time, with its presbyters as the guardians of this "remaining" (Acts 20:17–38).[19] In this context it is not necessary to develop a detailed theory of the Church's teaching office centered on the teaching office of the successor of Peter, although it would not be difficult to indicate the New Testament lines running in this direction. (On the one hand there is the ever-clearer idea of tradition and succession and on the other hand the development of Petrine theology.) It is manifest that the fundamental content of apostolic succession consists precisely in the authority to preserve apostolic faith; also, that the plenitude of teaching authority that goes with this includes the task of making concrete the moral demands of grace and

[19] In this connection, cf. F. Mussner, "Die *Una Sancta* nach Apg 2:42", in *Praesentia salutis* (Düsseldorf, 1967), 212–222.

of working them out in detail with regard to the contemporary situation.[20]

Thus, our reflections have returned to their starting point. Christian faith does indeed involve a praxis on the part of faith; orthodoxy without orthopraxy fails to reach the core of the Christian reality, namely, love proceeding from grace. This also implies that Christian praxis is nourished by the core of Christian faith, that is, the grace that appeared in Christ and that is appropriated in the sacrament of the Church. Faith's praxis depends on faith's truth, in which man's truth is made visible and lifted up to a new level by God's truth. Hence, it is fundamentally opposed to a praxis that first wants to produce facts and so establish truth. By holding on to the Creator, faith's praxis protects the creation against such a total manipulation of reality. By looking to the example of Jesus Christ, faith recognizes fundamental human values and rescues them from all manipulation. It protects man by protecting creation; the apostles' successors have an indestructible commission to maintain apostolic teaching and make it present. Since grace refers to both the creation and the Creator, apostolic exhortation (as a continuation of Old Testament admonitions) is involved with

[20] Cf. L. Bouyer, *L'Église de Dieu. Corps du Christ et temple de l'Esprit* (Paris, 1970), 401–447; Y. Congar, *Ministères et communion ecclésiale* (Paris, 1971), 51–94.

human reason. Contrary to appearances, the flight into pure orthopraxy, as well as the attempt to banish substantive morals from the realm of faith (with the teaching authority that is an integral part of the realm of faith), turn reason into a heresy. In the one case reason's ability to recognize truth is denied, and the renunciation of truth is elevated into a method; and in the other case faith is lifted out of the realm of reason, and rational considerations are not admitted as being possible components of the world of faith. Either faith is declared to be irrational, or reason is made out to be unbelieving—or both. On the one hand reason is imagined to speak with a single voice at any one time—which, of itself, it cannot do—and on the other hand its message is bound to what is contemporary in such a way that truth disappears behind the values of the age. Thus, every age sees reason differently, which ultimately leads to opting for the absolute dominance of the practical reason. The faith of the apostles, as we see it in Romans 1 and 2 for instance, thinks more highly of reason. This faith is convinced that reason is capable of embracing truth, and that, therefore, faith does not have to erect its edifice apart from the tradition of reason, but finds its language in communication with the reason of the nations through a process of reception and dialectic. This means that both the process of assimilation and that of negation and criticism must be pursued on the basis of faith's fundamental options and must be firmly rooted in the latter. Reason's ability to embrace truth also implies that truth's content is constant and coincident with the constancy of faith.

The task of the Church's teaching office in moral matters follows automatically from what has been said. As we have seen, faith involves fundamental decisions (with definite content) in moral matters. The first obligation of the teaching office is to continue the apostolic exhortation and to protect these fundamental decisions against reason's capitulation to the age, as well as against reason's capitulation in the face of almighty praxis. There must be a correspondence with basic insights of human reason, albeit these insights have been purified, deepened and broadened through contact with the way of faith. As we have said, the positive, critical dialogue with reason is something that must go on for all time. On the one hand there is never a clear-cut division between genuine reason and what merely appears "reasonable"; on the other hand the two things coexist in all ages, that is, the "appearance" of reason and the manifestation of truth through reason. The whole Church is involved in the process of assimilating what is genuinely rational and rejecting what is only superficially reasonable. It cannot be done by an isolated teaching authority, with oracular infallibility in every detail. The life and suffering of Christians, living out their faith in the midst of the times, is just as much a part of it as the reflections and questionings of the scholars. Indeed, the latter is nothing but idle verbiage unless it is backed up by a Christian existence that has learned to discern the spirits in the "Passion" of everyday life. The faith experience of the whole Church and the research and questioning, in faith, on the part of scholars, represent two factors; a third factor is the watchful attention, listening and deciding undertaken by the teaching authority. Right from the first century it has been the Church's experience that there is nothing automatic about the maintenance of right doctrine; responsible shepherds are needed in the Church to "exhort and admonish". That is why it has fashioned the office of those who are called, through prayer and the imposition of hands, to be successors of the apostles. Today equally, this office is indispensable. Those who fundamentally deny that it has any competence to make detailed and practical decisions for or against an interpretation on the morality that springs from grace are trying to overturn the very basic form of apostolic tradition.

Hans Urs von Balthasar

Nine Propositions on Christian Ethics

Preliminary note

The Christian who lives by faith has the right to justify his moral actions on the basis of his faith. Since faith's content—namely, Jesus Christ, the revealer of a love that is triune and divine—has adopted both the form and the guilt of the First Adam, as well as the constrictions, perplexities and crises of the latter's existence, the Christian is in no danger of failing to find the First Adam, and hence his own ethical problems, in the Second. Jesus, for instance, had to choose between his Father and his family: "Son, why have you treated us so?" (Lk 2:48). So the Christian will make the weighty decisions of his life from the perspective of Christ, that is, of faith. It would be wrong to use the term "ethics from above" for an ethics that sets out from the full brilliance of the light of revelation and works backward to the fumbling preliminary stages, as opposed to an ethics "from below", which takes anthropology as its foundation.

Nor can this ethics be accused of being unhistorical in that it gives the Gospel precedence over Old Testament law. The path is determined and illuminated by the goal one has in view, and this applies particularly to this unique path of salvation history, which only attains its goal as a result of the dialectic between, on the one hand, discontinuity and, on the other hand, a fulfillment going beyond all expectation (cf. Paul in particular) and inner fulfillment (cf. Matthew and James). Naturally, from a chronological point of view, propositions 5 and 6 should come before the christological ones, and propositions 7 and 9 before the latter. But the Christian lives in the "last age" and must continually strive beyond those elements within him that are preliminary and seek to embrace things of ultimate validity. Thus, it is more (not less) necessary for Christ, too, to live out his obedience to the Father, not merely at the level of prophetic immediacy, but by keeping the law and by "faith" in the promise. And the Christian follows him in this.

The following propositions are highly summary in form and leave many essential matters undiscussed. Thus the Church, for instance, is only referred to obliquely; there is no mention of her sacraments, of the relationship to her official authority. Similarly, there is no discussion of the casuistic decisions, with their wide implications, that face today's Church, decisions that she must take in the context of humanity as a whole.

I

The Fulfillment of Ethics in Christ

1. Christ as the Concrete Norm

Christian ethics must be modeled on Jesus Christ since, as the Son of the Father, he carried out the entire will of God (i.e., every "ought") in the world. He did this "for us", so that from him, the fulfilled concrete norm of all ethical actions, we might receive the freedom to fulfill God's will and to live according to our nature as free children of the Father.

1. Christ is the concrete categorical imperative. He is the formally universal norm of ethical action, applicable to everyone. But he is also the personal and concrete norm, who, in virtue of his suffering for us and his eucharistic surrender of his life for us (which imparts it to us—*per ipsum et in ipso*), empowers us inwardly to do the Father's will together with him (*cum ipso*). The imperative is based on the indicative (Rom 6:7ff., 2 Cor 5:15, etc.)—but the Father's will is both: to love his children in him and with him (1 Jn 5:1f.) and to worship in spirit and in truth (Jn 4:23). Christ's life is at the same time deed and cult, and this achieved

unity is normative for the Christian. Only in infinite reverence (Phil 2:12) can we participate in the saving work of God, whose absolute love towers infinitely above us—in the *maior dissimilitudo*. Leiturgia is inseparable from ethical conduct.

2. The Christian imperative lifts us beyond the problems involved in autonomy and heteronomy:

a. because while the Son of God, begotten of the Father, is *"heteros"* vis-à-vis him, he is not *"heteron"*. As God he responds autonomously to his Father (his Person coincides with his "procession", i.e., his "mission"), whereas as man he possesses the divine will and his own affirmation of it as the ground of his existence (Heb 10:5f.; Phil 2:6f.) and the inner source of his personal action (Jn 4:34, etc.), even when it comes to suffering the opposition that sinners offer to God.

(N.b.: where Christ's divinity is not recognized, he necessarily appears as a human exemplar, and Christian ethics becomes either heteronomous, where Christ becomes simply an obligatory norm for my conduct, or autonomous, to the extent that his actions are interpreted merely as the achieved self-perfection of the human ethical subject.)

b. because we are empowered, by the Son's Eucharist, by means of which we are born with him, by grace, from the Father's loins, and by the communication to us (creatures, "*heteron*", as we are) of the Spirit common to them both, to develop a sphere of free action that is distinctively our own. Thus, our "drink" becomes a "spring" within us (Jn 4:13f.; 7:38). And since God acts "gratis" in his grace, and we ought also to act "gratis" in love (Mt 10:8; Lk 14:12–14), the "great reward in heaven" (Lk 6:23) cannot be anything other than love itself. In the eternal plan of God (Eph 1:1–10) the final goal coincides with the first stimulus to our freedom (*interior intimo meo*, cf. Rom 8:15f., 26f.).

3. It follows that all Christian action is a privilege, not an obligation, since we are God's children. More precisely, for Christ, the whole weight of his sense of constraint ("must"—the Greek *dei*), right up to the Cross, rests on his awareness of being absolutely free to manifest the Father's saving will. Often enough for us sinners, the privilege of being children of God takes on a crucifying aspect, both in personal decisions and in the context of the community of the Church; for the Church's precepts are intended to lead the believer out of the alienation of sin to his true identity and freedom, whereas they can (and often must) seem hard and legalistic to those who are imperfect, just as the Father's will seemed to the Crucified.

2. The Universality of the Concrete Norm

The norm provided by Christ's concrete existence is personal and, as such, universal, since he makes the Father's love comprehensively and completely present to the world; he embraces all the differences between human beings and their ethical situations and unites all persons (in their uniqueness and freedom) in his own Person, having authority over them in the Holy Spirit of freedom in order to lead them all into the Father's kingdom.

1. Christ's concrete existence—his life, suffering, death and ultimate bodily resurrection—surpasses all other systems of ethical norms. In the final analysis it is to this norm alone, which is itself the prototype of perfect obedience to God the Father, that the moral conduct of Christians has to answer. Christ's existence transcends the difference between those who have the "law" (Jews) and those "without the law" (Gentiles) (1 Cor 9:20f.), between servant and master, man and woman (Gal 3:28), and so forth. In Christ all have been endowed with the same freedom of children and heirs, and all are striving toward the same goal. The "new" commandment of Jesus (Jn 13:34)—which, since it is fulfilled christologically, goes beyond the chief commandment of the Old Covenant (Dt 6:4ff.)—is more than the sum of the individual prescriptions

and applications of the "Ten Words". The synthesis of the Father's entire will that is achieved in the Person of Christ is eschatological and unsurpassable. Hence, a priori, it is universally normative.

2. Insofar as Christ is the incarnate Word and Son of God the Father, he transcends in himself the clear separation into two sides that characterizes the Old Testament "covenant". He is more than the "mediator" who comes between the two parties; he is their personified encounter, and hence he is "One": "Now an intermediary implies more than one; but God is one" (Gal 3:20). The Church of Christ is nothing other than the fullness of this "One"; it is his "Body", enlivened by him (Eph 1:22f.), his "Bride" to the extent that he is "one flesh" (Eph 5:29) or "one spirit" (1 Cor 6:17) with it. Even understood as the "People of God", the Church is no longer a plurality, but "you are all one in Christ Jesus" (Gal 3:28). Because Jesus acted "for all", life within his community is both personalizing and socializing.

3. The fact that the action of the Cross has taken place for us without our active cooperation (". . . one has died for all; therefore all have died . . . that those who live might live no longer for themselves", 2 Cor 5:14f.), the fact that we have been

inserted "into Christ", does not constitute alienation for us; we have been "transplanted" from the
"darkness" of our sinful, alienated being into the
truth and freedom of the children of God (Col
1:13), for whose sake we were created (Eph 1:4ff.).
On the basis of the Cross we have been given the
Holy Spirit of Christ and of God (Rom 8:9, 11);
thus, both Christ's Person and work are at all
times present and operative in us, and we too are
continually made present in Christ.

This mutual inherence has an explicitly ecclesial
dimension for the believer. For, as a result of the
outpouring of the Holy Spirit of Father and Son—
the Spirit of the divine "We"—into the hearts of
believers, this "being-for-one-another" that is the
meaning of Jesus' new commandment is an even
more fundamental a priori assumption (Rom 5:5).
At the more-than-organic—that is, the personal
—level of the Church, our membership in the "one
body" means that we are given a personal awareness of being a "we"; implementing it in terms of
life is the Christian's ethical task. So the Church is
open to the world, just as Christ is to the Father
and his all-embracing kingdom (1 Cor 15:24);
both "mediate" only in the sense of that *immediacy*
that determines every last detail of life in the
Church.

3. The Christian Meaning of The "Golden Rule"

The "Golden Rule" (Mt 7:12; Lk 6:31) in the mouth of Christ and in the context of the Sermon on the Mount can only be described as summing up the law and the prophets, because it bases what the members of Christ may expect from and render to one another on the gift of God (i.e., Christ). Thus, it goes beyond mere humanitarianism and involves the interpersonal exchange of divine life.

1. In Matthew and (even more explicitly) in Luke, the "Golden Rule" is situated in the context of the Beatitudes, the renunciation of retributive justice, the love of one's enemies, and the command to be "perfect" and "merciful" like the Father in heaven. Thus, the gift that the Father gives is seen to be what one member of Christ can expect from another and so must give in return. This once more demonstrates that both the "law" and general "humanitarianism" have always had their "goal" (Rom 10:4) in Christ.

2. The "law" itself was not merely an expression of a humanitarian ethos, but a proclamation of the saving faithfulness of God, who wanted to enter a covenant with the people (cf. proposition 6). How-

ever, the "prophets" looked to a fulfillment of the law that would not be possible until God removed all heteronomy and set his law in the form of his Spirit deep in the hearts of men (Jer 31:33; Ezek 36:26f.).

3. In Christian terms no personal or social ethics can be envisaged apart from God's effectual and bountiful invitation to man. Dialogue between human beings, if it is to be morally in order, presupposes a dialogue between God and man, whether or not man is explicitly aware of this. Conversely, however, man's relationship to God points expressly to the dialogue, at a new and higher level, between Jew and Gentile, master and servant, man and woman, parents and children, poor and rich, and so on.

All Christian ethics is therefore cruciform—that is, vertical and horizontal—but this "shape" cannot for a moment be abstracted from its concrete content; namely, from him who stands, crucified, between God and man. It is he who makes himself present as the sole norm in every particular relationship, in every situation. "All things are lawful for me" (1 Cor 6:12; cf. Rom 14–15), so long as I remember that my freedom arises from my belonging to Christ (1 Cor 6:19; cf. 3:21–23).

4. Sin

*It is only where God's love goes "to the end" that
human guilt manifests itself as sin, its inner disposition
arising from a spirit that is positively inimical to God.*

1. The uniqueness and concreteness of the personal moral norm implies that all moral guilt, like
it or not, must be referred to Christ, is responsible
before him and must be borne by him on the
Cross. It is because the Christian, with his moral
conduct, is so close to the principle of divine
holiness that animates him as a Christian, that
guilt becomes *sin*, as compared to the infringe-
ment of a mere "law" (in Judaism) or a mere
"idea" (in Greek thought). The holiness of the
Holy Spirit in Christ/Church convicts the world
of its sin (Jn 16:8–11), a world of which we too are
a part ("If we say that we have not sinned, we
make God a liar", 1 Jn 1:10).

2. The presence of absolute love in the world
deepens man's guilty No and makes it a demonic
No, more negative than man appreciates, that
tries to draw man into the anti-Christian current
(cf. the apocalyptic beasts, Paul on the powers of
the cosmos, 1 Jn, etc.). The individual has to do
his part in the battle of Christ/Church by fighting

equipped with "the whole armor of God" (Eph 6:11). The demonic expresses itself above all in a loveless, self-glorifying gnosis that claims to be as coextensive as the agape that works God's will (Gen 3:5). Yet this gnosis "puffs up" (1 Cor 8:1) instead of building up. Since it will not accept the personal, concrete norm, it portrays sin as mere guilt, the result of a violation of a law or an idea, and it endeavors increasingly to exculpate it through psychology, sociology and other similar means.

3. The sword-point of anti-Christian sin is directly aimed at the center of the personal norm. It pierces the heart of the Crucified, which represents the concreteness, in the world, of trinitarian love in its self-surrender. How the Crucified Son can take sin upon himself remains a mystery of faith that no philosophy can pronounce to be either "necessary" or "impossible". For the same reason, the verdict on sin is reserved to the pierced Son of Man, to whom "all judgment is given" (Jn 5:22). "Judge not" (Mt 7:1).

The Old Testament Elements of the Synthesis to Come

5. The Promise (Abraham)

The moral subject (Abraham) is constituted by the call of God and by obedience to this call (Heb 11:8).

1. Following the act of obedience, the inner meaning of the call shows itself to be an unimaginable, universal promise ("all nations", yet concentrated in a personal way: semini tuo, *Gal 3:16). The name of him who is obedient is identical with his mission (Gen 17:1–8); since both promise and fulfillment come from God, Abraham is given a supernatural fruitfulness.*

2. Obedience is faith in God and hence the appropriate response (Gen 15:6), involving not only the spirit, but the flesh also (Gen 17:13). Thus, obedience must go to the lengths of giving back the fruit that grace had bestowed (Gen 22).

3. Abraham exists in an obedience that, looking up to the (unattainable) stars, awaits what has been promised.

On 1: All biblical ethics is based on the call of the personal God and man's believing response. God describes himself in his call to man as the One who is faithful, truthful, just, merciful (and other paraphrases of his Name), and it is on the basis of this Name that the name of the one who responds (i.e., his unique personality) is determined. The call isolates the subject in preparation for this encounter (Abraham must leave clan and homeland), and in facing the call ("Here am I", Gen 22:1) he is given his mission, which becomes a norm for his conduct henceforth. In the solitary dialogue–encounter with God, Abraham, in virtue of his mission, becomes the founder of a community whose laws governing horizontal relationships all depend, in the biblical testimony, on the founder's or mediator's vertical relationship with God or on God's founding act (Ex 22:20; 23:9; Dt 5:14f.; 15:12–18; 16:11f.; 24:17f.). The latter is grace without measure; it cannot be manipulated and remains the plumb line for all man's doings (cf. Jesus' parable of the unmerciful servant, Mt 18:21ff.). The unlimited quality of the blessing promised to Abraham is understood more and more clearly in the Old Covenant as its openness to messianic fulfillment; the intensifying movement toward Jesus Christ and the imparting (through faith in him) of the Holy Spirit goes hand in hand with the opening up of the promise to the "nations" (Gal 3:14).

On 2: The "covenant" (Gen 15:18, etc.), established by God's call and faith's response, addresses the moral subject in all the dimensions of his life, that is, in the risk of faith, but also in the flesh and its possibilities ("So shall my covenant be in your flesh an everlasting covenant" Gen 17:13). And, lest the Isaac who was born by God's power should ever be regarded as an end in himself, God asks for him back. If the faith of the sterile man was faith in a God "who gives life to the dead and calls into existence the things that do not exist" (Rom 4:17), the faith of the father who gives back the son of the promise is an active resurrection faith: "He considered that God was able to raise him even from the dead" (Heb 11:19).

On 3: The existence of Abraham (and hence of the entire Old Covenant, including the period of the law) can only be a clinging to God by faith without being able to change God's promise into fulfillment. The ancient people can only "wait" (Heb 11:10) and "seek" (11:14), having seen the promise and "greeted it from afar", acknowledging that "they were strangers and exiles on the earth" (11:13–14). It was precisely in their intermediate state, not being able to reach what was promised and yet persisting in waiting for it, that the ancients were commended by God (*martyrēthentes*, 11:39). This is of importance for what follows.

6. The Law

*The giving of the law at Sinai goes beyond the promise
to Abraham in that—though in a provisional manner,
from "outside" and from "above"—it expressly reveals
God's inner disposition in order to deepen the covenant
response to him: "You shall be holy, for I am holy".
This "You shall", which originates in God's inner
nature, has man's inner disposition in view. The absolute truthfulness of the God who offers man this covenant
(Rom 7:12) assures man that it is possible to respond
and correspond to this "You shall". For the present,
however, this truthfulness is not matched by the same
absolute truthfulness on the part of man; it is only latent
in the promise (to Abraham) that is announced in a new
and more precise form as a prophetic promise.*

1. The law is subsequent to the promise and does
not abrogate it in its implications (Rom 7; Gal 3);
thus, it can only be intended as a more detailed
definition of faith's "waiting" attitude. It illuminates from various angles the attitude of the man
who is "righteous before God". This attitude no
doubt corresponds to the constitutive structure of
human nature ("natural law"), because God is not
only Creator but the continual Giver of blessing.
But the theme of this righteousness is not man
himself, but the deeper unveiling of God's holiness

in his covenant faithfulness. Hence, it is not a case of "imitating" (the nature of) God in the Greek sense, but of responding to his attitude as manifested in his "great deeds" toward Israel. Since, however, the perfect response remains the subject of the promise, the law remains dialectical in the sense described by Paul: it is good in itself, but yields transgression, and to that extent it is both negatively and positively a "tutor" (*paidagogos*) leading to Christ.

2. From God's perspective the law's imperative offers the opportunity of living in a godly way before him in the proximity created by the covenant. Yet this gracious offer is only the first act of a saving drama that is only consummated in Christ; initially, in indicating the precise shape of the response that God expects (the positive side), the drama only serves to uncover man's inability to respond (the negative side). Thus, the promise still awaits fulfillment. The yawning gap between the two can only be faced in an attitude of waiting, in the patience of a faith that hopes; man, however, feels such waiting to be unbearable and attempts two different shortcuts:

a. By elevating the law (the Torah) into an abstract absolute that takes the place of the living God. By trying to fulfill the abstract letter literally, the Pharisee imagines he can manufacture the elusive response. This erection of an abstract, formal imperative has given rise to many forms of ethics; for example, the neo-Kantian realm of "absolute validities" or "values", the structuralist and phenomenological ethics (Scheler), which all tend to set up the human subject as his own lawgiver, as an autonomous subject along Idealist lines, accepting limitation in order to realize himself—such as we find in Kant's ethical formalism.

b. By taking the law, which is felt to be a foreign body, and dissolving it into the flux of the movement of promise and hope. The law, externally imposed and producing an inner sense of guilt (Kafka), cannot emanate from a faithful and merciful God, but only from a tyrannical demiurge (hence, E. Bloch's pact with gnosis; cf. Freud's "superego"), who must be rejected as a delusion belonging to the past, on the basis of a hope arising from man's own autonomous source.

c. Both escape routes are combined in dialectical materialism, which identifies law with the dialectical movement of history and so dissolves it. Marx knows that it is not the negative abolition of the law ("communism") that brings the desired reconciliation, but only positive humanism, which causes the law to coincide with freedom's spontaneity (in an atheistic parallel to Jer 31 and Ezek 34). Here (as in its modern distortions), corresponding to the provisional character of Old Testament ethics in view of eschatological Christian ethics, transcendental "reconciliation" stays at the level of immanent political "liberation", and its subject is primarily the people, the human collective, and not the person; for it is only in Christ that the uniqueness of the person shines forth.

3. Where Christian faith in the promise fulfilled in Christ disappears, historical influence on mankind passes not so much to extrabiblical, fragmentary ethics, as to the Old Testament ethics that is closest to Christian ethics. Moreover, since there is some awareness of the fulfillment in Christ, what we find is an absolutist caricature of Old Testament ethics; that is, a law and a prophecy that are posited as absolute.

III

Fragments of Extrabiblical Ethics

7. Conscience

*1. Man, that is to say, extrabiblical man, is awakened
to a theoretical/practical self-awareness thanks to a
voluntary and loving challenge on the part of his fellow
man. In responding, he experiences (in the* cogito/sum*)
both the radiance of reality as such (which is true and
good), manifesting itself and beckoning man toward it,
as well as the fact that his freedom is part of his
relationship to his fellow men.*[1]

*2. Man's whole constitution is unconditionally (*neces-
sitate naturalis inclinationis: de Ver 22, 5*) predis-
posed toward goodness as it reveals itself in a light of
transcendence (*synderesis, primal conscience*). He tends
toward it in some way even in the sensual parts of his
spirit-directed nature.*

*Man cannot be prevented from following, albeit
covertly, the light that beckons to him, neither by its
eventual withdrawal, nor by being distracted by immediately available goods, nor even when the gift quality
of the good is obscured by sin. Thus, even pagans will be*

[1] Cf. Hansjürgen Verweyen, *Ontologische Voraussetzungen
des Glaubensaktes* (Patmos, 1969).

96

judged by Jesus Christ "according to my gospel" (Rom 2:16).

3. Abstract formulations of man's attraction to the good in terms of "natural law"—for example, the "categorical imperative" governing relations between fellow men—are derivative and point toward their source.

On 1: Summoned by his fellow men, man awakes to the *cogito/sum* in that he identifies subsistent radiance with reality. But since this awakening is something he has been given, he does not experience the identity as absolute; it too is something given. Three things are observable simultaneously in this transcendental "opening":

a. The "givenness" of the absolute identity of spirit and being, and hence of absolute self-possession in plenitude and freedom. This "givenness" enables us to share in it (and this absolute "we call God, *qui interius docet, inquantum huiusmodi lumen animae infundit*": Thomas, *de An* 5 ad 6).

b. In awakening to this self-disclosing "givenness", man observes the difference and distance between freedom as absolute and freedom as gift. Thus, he is attracted to respond freely to the absolute gift.

c. The call that comes from the absolute is identical, transcendentally speaking, with that which comes from one's fellow man, but differentiation occurs a posteriori in view of the realization that one's fellow man, too, has "only" been awakened in the same manner. All the same, the original transcendental unity of both challenges that call to man is shown to be indivisible.

On 2: Freedom, understood as autonomy, and grace, which grants participation in itself (*diffusivum sui*) are side by side in the original identity of being and radiance (the absolutely free and hence good— and hence *fascinosum*, beautiful). Similarly, in the awakened, dependent identity, freedom and inclination (toward the primal Good) are inseparable. The active attraction of the unconditionally good imparts to the act of free response an element of "passivity" that does not interfere with its freedom (*S. Th.* I 80, 2; *de Ver* 25, 1; 22, 13, 4).

The whole man is permeated by this predisposition to submit to the power of the good, and this includes his senses, informed as they are by spirit. (Though the senses, abstracted from the human totality, cannot manage to perceive the good in itself, but treat particular goods as ends.) The distinctive ethical task laid upon man is that of ethicizing (*ethizesthai*) his entire spiritual-bodily nature; success is called virtue. This is all the more the case when his fellow man obliges him to allow his freedom to be defined by, and to define, other, equally embodied freedoms, a task that must be carried out under the illumination of the good and always requires the material vehicle to be shot through with luminosity.

In fact, the original "opening" of the good in itself, on the basis of the *cogito/sum* (or the transparency of the *imago Dei* as it reveals its exemplar), is not something that lasts. All the same, it stays in the mind *"tamquam nota artificis operi suo impressa"* (Descartes, *Med* III). Since it has been a factor in the spirit's initial coming to itself, it cannot be completely forgotten, even when the person concerned has consciously or habitually turned away from the light of the good in order to pursue particular things for enjoyment or utility. Furthermore, it constitutes at least a transcendental intimation of what revelation is and is the constant source of "positive" revelation, of both Old and New Covenants, for the whole of mankind. However, when this revelation proceeds from the a posteriori realm of history, we must not forget that the summons that comes from our fellow man has the same (transcendental and dialogical) origin as the call of the good in itself, pure and simple. Only the *magister interior* can judge how far and how clearly such "positive" revelation is actually at work outside the biblical field, but according to Paul this *magister* judges even the hearts of Gentiles by the adequately explicit norm of God's self-giving in Jesus Christ.

On 3: "Signposts" are provided against the time when there will be an obscuring of the original brilliance of the Good (under the form of grace and love) that looks for the free response of loving gratitude. As such, these signposts do not replace the Good in itself, nor yet do they represent it; they only call it to mind. Insofar as they refer to the most important situations of incarnated and socially constituted spirit, they develop along the lines of "natural law". This must not be divinized; if it is not to ossify, it must clearly preserve its essentially relative character as a pointer, indicating the vitality and self-giving nature of the Good. This also applies to Kant's categorical imperative: because of its formalism, it is obliged to oppose abstract "duty" against the "inclination" of the senses, whereas in reality it is a question of encouraging the person's absolute "inclination" toward absolute good to triumph over contrary particular affections. What man appropriates to himself with a view to the absolute norm (*oikeiosis*, in Stoic terms) coincides with self-expropriation in favor of the divine good and the good of one's fellow man.

8. The Prebiblical Natural Order

Where there is no self-revelation on the part of a free, personal God, man tries to find his life's moral order in the surrounding cosmos. Since he owes his existence to cosmic laws, it is natural for thought about origins (i.e., the divine) to be fused in his mind with thought about the natural realm. This kind of theo-cosmological ethics collapses when the biblical fact attains resonance in world history.

1. A prebiblical ethics taking its bearings by *physis* can inquire into the good (*honestum*) appropriate to human nature by analogy with the good of natural things. This human good, however, will be part of an all-embracing world order that, while it has an absolute (divine) dimension and hence gives scope for ordered moral action, retains a worldly and finite dimension and to that extent hinders human freedom of decision from attaining its full stature. Thus, the goals of action remain partly political (in the context of a micro- or macropolis) and partly individualistic and intellectualist insofar as *theoria* and knowledge of the rhythms of the universe seem to be the most desirable aim.

2. Once the biblical fact has come into view, on the free initiative of God—who is radically distinct from created nature—man is raised to a freedom that can no longer take its pattern of behavior from subhuman nature. If this freedom will not render thanks to the God of grace in the Christian understanding, it will logically seek its source in

itself. It will understand ethical action as self-legislation, initially, perhaps, recapitulating earlier patterns of cosmology (cf. Spinoza, Goethe, Hegel) and ultimately jettisoning this preliminary stage (cf. Feuerbach, Nietzsche).

3. The development that has gone on is irreversible. Even though there may be a tendency to let Christian ethics slip back into its preparatory Old Testament form (cf. 6, 3 above), we can also observe how a Christian light has irradiated non-biblical religions and ethical systems (cf. the growth of the social component in India: Tagore, Gandhi). Our drawing of a distinction between existential and explicit dogmatic knowledge once again invites the warning, "Judge not."

9. Post-Christian Anthropological Ethics

The attempt to find a basis for a post-Christian and non-Christian ethics can only be pursued in the dialogical relationship of human freedoms ("I–Thou", "I–We"). But since in this case the cultic attitude of thanksgiving (to God) no longer forms part of the free person's primal act, the reciprocal gratitude between the subjects becomes a secondary and only relatively valid act; the reciprocal limitation of free subjects who are per se unlimited appears extrinsic and imposed. It is impossible to achieve a synthesis between the fulfillment of the individual and that of the community.

1. The human "nature" or "structure" that remains in a post-Christian stage is constituted by the reciprocity of freedoms, where each freedom is only awakened and aroused to respond (and to issue a challenge in turn) by some other freedom. We seem to be back at the "Golden Rule". However, because the particular freedom addressed cannot simply acknowledge its debt to the fellow freedom that has elicited it (otherwise it would be ultimately heteronomous), and since God's challenge, which grounds both freedoms, is denied, the degree of give and take and self-surrender on the part of each of them is limited and calculated. Either intersubjectivity is seen as a secondary (and obscure) mode of the one sovereign subject, or else the subjects remain monads, impenetrable to one another.

2. The so-called "anthropological sciences" can bring valuable individual insights to the phenomenon of human life, but they are powerless to remedy this fundamental weakness in a society conceived simply in terms of an aggregate of fellow human beings.

3. This anthropological powerlessness is most clearly apparent when death destroys the possibility of a synthesis between the individual's personal fulfillment and his social integration. The two torsos of meaning, which had begun to be developed separately, remain unconnected, making it impossible to construct a self-evident intramundane ethics; for, in the face of death's meaninglessness—and hence the meaninglessness of a life that is doomed to die—man can refuse to entertain ethical norms at all. The only place where these two lines converge is in the resurrection of Christ, which guarantees and anticipates the fulfillment both of the individual and of the community of the Church. Through the latter, in fact, the fulfillment of the world is also guaranteed in such a way that, without bringing the world to an end, God can be "all in all".